The Real Coach K

The Real Coach K

◆

Still Having Fun after Forty-four Years of Coaching!

John "Coach K" Kaminsky

iUniverse

The Real Coach K
Still Having Fun after Forty-four Years of Coaching!

Copyright © 2007 John Kaminsky.

All rights reserved. No part of this book may be used or reproduced by any means, graphic, electronic, or mechanical, including photocopying, recording, taping or by any information storage retrieval system without the written permission of the author except in the case of brief quotations embodied in critical articles and reviews.

iUniverse books may be ordered through booksellers or by contacting:

iUniverse
1663 Liberty Drive
Bloomington, IN 47403
www.iuniverse.com
844-349-9409

Because of the dynamic nature of the Internet, any web addresses or links contained in this book may have changed since publication and may no longer be valid. The views expressed in this work are solely those of the author and do not necessarily reflect the views of the publisher, and the publisher hereby disclaims any responsibility for them.

Any people depicted in stock imagery provided by Getty Images are models, and such images are being used for illustrative purposes only. Certain stock imagery © Getty Images.

ISBN: 978-0-5954-6009-0 (sc)

Print information available on the last page.

iUniverse rev. date: 09/02/2020

"Coach K led us with an enthusiastic passion for the game of basketball. He made the game fun and exciting.
Not many coaches have participated in warmups with their players to the sounds of 'Sweet Georgia Brown'.
His love for the game was only exceeded by the love he gave to his family and teams."
—Bob Weldon, Millersport High School, Class of 1977

"Through all his years of coaching, Coach K has had the ability to take his tremendous enthusiasm and passion for the game of basketball and pass it on to his players. All the while, reminding them that basketball IS a game, and that faith and family come first."
—Jeff Stought, Former Player

"From the day I met Coach K in 1989, he has been one of the most influential people I have met. Not only did he teach you the X's and O's of basketball, he taught you the X's and O's of life. His love for basketball can only be outdone by his love for his family."
—Rob Smith, Former Player at OSU Newark, 1990–1993

First and foremost, I dedicate this book, with love, to Karen Virginia Kaminsky.
Every word in this book is dedicated to her. She is the best person I have met while I have been here on earth.

I would also like to dedicate this book to my wonderful, caring children: Becky, Jeff, and Brett

Contents

Introduction . . . . *xi*
Go Man Go 1
Last Man Warming Up 7
Enthusiasm Creates Momentum 15
Play the Best, Beat the Rest 33
Not Finished Yet! 51
Epilogue 59

Introduction

I have always considered myself the Rodney Dangerfield of coaching. As Rodney so famously stated, "I get no respect." But I have always found ways to motivate my kids and teams, and would have them ready to play every game. The Lord has been very good to me during my seventy-one years. If I had to prioritize my life, I would put it in this order: first and foremost, the Lord, who has guided my path through life; second, my family, which has supported and loved me through all the ups and downs of coaching; and third, basketball. Basketball means so much to me not only because of the sport, but because of the students and players. Passing on my love of the game has been a wonderful experience and always a challenge. I have had many moments where I have been proud of the students I coach, no matter what the outcome of the game was; I have witnessed miracles both on the court and in my life. Also, I have had those not-so-great moments where I acted in a way that I am not proud of. When I set out to write my memoir, I made a conscious decision to include all of these moments, good and bad, because they make my life what it is. Even as I wrote this book, I continued to learn about myself and my career as a coach. I hope that I can pass on to others some of the lessons I learned as a soldier, a basketball player, a coach, and a father.

Go Man Go

I was born in Republic, Pennsylvania on September 9, 1936. My mother's maiden name was Elizabeth Chelsea Guerrierri. She hung wallpaper and cleaned houses in our community for twenty years. My father, John Joseph Kaminsky, worked as a coal miner for twenty-eight years and served as a constable and chief of our local police department.

When I was about five years old, I remember sneaking out of bed late at night after my mom and dad went to sleep. I would put a paper cup up above the doorway in the living room and practice shooting. In those days, we did not have any little league programs. My friends and I would play basketball any place we could find some type of hoop. We even made our own hoops by nailing bushel baskets to boards.

When I was a freshman in high school playing in the Redstone High School varsity basketball game, I got a nickname that stuck. I was incredibly skinny, and I loved to dribble and clown around with the ball. While I was on the sideline, I would let the ball go around my neck and down my arms. Father Noroski, a priest, was at the game and announced, "John looks like a snake out there on the floor!" From that day on, my teammates, the priests, and my coach called me "Snake."

I had a job working at the local movie theater making popcorn and carrying in the films when they were delivered. My pay was $7.50 a week, plus all the popcorn I could eat. One weekend, the theater was showing the movie *Go Man Go*. It is a great film about Meadow Lark Lemon and the beginning of the Harlem Globetrotters. I watched it twice on Friday night, three times on Saturday, and three times on Sunday. I saw over and over how much fun Meadow Lark Lemon and his Globetrotters had playing the game. I admired what those players could do with a basketball and wanted to be just as good as those Globetrotters. From that weekend on, I practiced my ball handling and dribbling and clowning, and I made basketball a special part of my life.

I graduated from high school in 1954, and like most of my friends, I did not want to spend my life in a coal mine. As much as I wanted a basketball scholarship, I did not think I was good enough. I figured I was only five-foot-ten, 139 pounds, weak, and slow, so I did not even bother to try out. The minimum age to volunteer for the draft was eighteen, and since I was only seventeen, I could not enlist unless my parents signed a permission form. So I talked my mom and dad into signing the papers and on August 23, 1954, I joined the United States Army.

I spent the first six months of basic training at Fort Knox, Kentucky, where I was also trained to be a radio operator in a tank. The Army then sent me to Fort Carson, Colorado for further training. After another six months, my orders came in stating I was to go to Frankfurt, Germany to join the 4th armored group at Gibbs Kaserne.

One of my worst fears in life is of water. I was hoping that I would fly to Germany, but of course, my orders stated that I was "to be shipped overseas on the troop ship the General William O. Darby." It took ten excruciatingly long days to cross the Atlantic Ocean. I prayed extra long and hard as we crossed the ocean. Many of the soldiers became seasick, but not me; I believe I was too scared to get sick.

When I arrived in Frankfurt, Germany in September of 1955, I was assigned to be a radio operator in a tank. They decided to take me out of being a radio operator and make me a field wireman instead. I knew I did not want to be a field wireman, so I immediately tried to find out how I could do something else. There was a position open supervising the gymnasium on the base. I was fortunate enough to get that job instead. My job entailed lining off the softball fields and taking care of and handing out equipment in the gymnasium. The job was similar to being a recreation director. This was the first time I had the privilege of coaching. I was given the job of player/coach of our base's team for basketball and softball. I had the opportunity to improve my basketball skills and travel throughout Germany playing ball for two seasons.

I left Frankfurt in July of 1957 to return to the United States, and to receive my discharge. On August 6, 1957, I headed home after three years serving my country. It seemed like everyone coming home was flying back, but not me; my orders stated that I would be shipped home on the troop ship, General William O. Darby—the same ship that had brought me to Germany two years earlier.

Coming home, it took eleven days because of storms and bad weather. Yes, I was scared, and yes, I cried every night hoping I would be able to kiss the ground someday. I should have known better and trusted the Lord more—he got me back home safe and sound.

On my way home from being discharged from Fort Dix, New Jersey, I decided to stop in a bar and have a cold beer while I was waiting for the train. To my surprise, they would not serve me because I was only twenty years old and considered underage. They were right not to serve me, but I was still upset thinking I had just served my country for three years, but I was not permitted to buy a beer.

The Korean War ended in 1953, before I enlisted, and the Vietnam War started in 1959, after I had been discharged. I was in college when the Vietnam War began. I was also married and had a daughter. Even though I was in the active reserves, the government did not call me back to active duty. Looking back on those years I feel very fortunate for missing both of those terrible wars, but if I had been called back to active duty, I would have been privileged to serve my country again.

Last Man Warming Up

After my tour of duty, I did not know what I was going to do next. I decided to go to a television repair school in Uniontown, Pennsylvania. My stay there did not last long—it wasn't what I really wanted to do. That all changed when a friend of mine, Buck Grover, needed a ride to visit a college in West Virginia to talk with the football coach about a scholarship.

Buck was by far the best athlete I knew growing up. Back when we were young, he was six-foot-five, about two hundred fifty pounds, and an exceptional athlete. After high school he accepted a scholarship to Clemson University for football. He played tight end, punted, and kicked field goals. He stayed there for one school year before returning home. The Chicago Cubs signed him to pitch in their farm system. With his bonus, he bought a red 1957 Chevrolet. He decided to come home one weekend, even after the Cubs's directors told him not to. Not only did he lose out on a great opportunity, but on the way home, he totaled his new car. In August of 1958, he asked me for a ride to Salem, West Virginia to talk to the football coach about a football scholarship. I had the day off and decided to take him to Salem. (He spent the next two years playing football at Salem College in Salem, West Virginia. He quit school and headed off to tryout kicking for the Pittsburgh Steelers. I feel he would have made it, but he got into a fight at a bar in Uniontown. Several fellows jumped him and he broke his leg in several places. His athletic opportunities were over. He passed away in 1996 because of a heart attack. May he rest in peace, Amen.)

While Buck was talking to the head football coach, I went into the gymnasium to watch their basketball team practice. That was when it hit me. I finally knew what I wanted to do—go to college, play basketball, and become a coach. I talked to the basketball coach, Mr. Clem Clower, and asked him if he needed any more players. Coach Clower told me that if I could make the team, he had a scholarship available.

I made the team, and during my freshmen year, Coach moved me into the starting lineup. We had two excellent shooters on our team, Fred Gandt and Dave Christe. One night in January of 1960, we were playing West Liberty College from Wheeling, West Virginia. We defeated them that night 120–97. That was a lot of scoring back in 1960. That was probably the best game I ever played in college. I scored twenty-nine points and pulled down thirty rebounds. Thirty rebounds is still a record at Salem College.

I show a copy of that newspaper article to my team at the start of every season—especially to our rebounders. I do not show them because I want to brag; rather I want to prove a point. I want to make them understand the importance of rebounding. I tell my players as I show them the article, "I was six-foot-two and 155 skinny pounds, weak, could not jump, could not dunk, but I did get thirty rebounds in one game because of positioning and timing."

During my freshman year at Salem, West Virginia I met a young lady, Karen Virginia Marks. She was a senior at Salem High School, and the daughter of the late Wilford "Duke" Marks and Blanche Nutter Marks. On our first date, I told Karen that we were going to get married. Three months later, right after she graduated from high school, we eloped and got married. Most of our friends said it would never last. As of June 8, 2007, we will have been married for forty-eight beautiful years. I honestly don't know how she has put up with me and my crazy coaching antics for the past forty-four years. She is a very special person.

Shortly after we got married, I met her parents. They took me in, and we lived with them until I graduated. I am very thankful for the way they accepted me into their family. Karen gave birth to our first child, Rebecca Lynn, on December 23rd, 1959. Our second child, Jeffrey Mark, was born on April 19, 1961. Our third child, Brett Alan, was born on April 23, 1965. I graduated from Salem College on

June 8, 1962, which was also our third wedding anniversary. I started teaching and coaching on September 4, 1962 at Oak Hill in Jackson County, Ohio. I was hired to teach government and history and serve as assistant football coach at Oak Hill High School. In the middle of the football season, the 8th grade basketball coach was talking about the low salary he would be getting for coaching junior high basketball—only one hundred fifty dollars for the season. He gave the impression that he did not want the position. I jumped at the opportunity to coach basketball and told him that I loved the game and would coach the team for free.

Oak Hill's gymnasium was an auditorium, and the gym floor was on a stage. Several times while we were practicing, I would look out in the auditorium and see the school superintendent, Dean Daugherty, sitting in the back row watching practice. The first thought that came to my mind was "Oh! Oh! I must be doing a poor job with the team."

Before the end of the season, I received a call from the superintendent. He was at a school board meeting, and he wanted to know if I would like to be the head basketball coach. The head coach at the time, Mr. Homer Williams, was going to accept the principal's position for the next school year, so the basketball position was open. Not needing any time to think about it, I accepted immediately. I was very appreciative and grateful for the opportunity. I also felt very proud of being offered the position over both the junior varsity and freshman coaches. I thought back to those days when Mr. Daugherty was watching practice in the auditorium and felt a lot better.

At Oak Hill High School during the 1964–65 season, we had a young man named Dan Brisker on our team. He stood about six feet tall and was an excellent outside shooter. That year Dan was a senior. He had an exceptional season scoring 550 points for a thirty-one points-per-game average. In those days we did not have the three-point field goal or his average could have been forty per game.

Another important thing I remember about Dan was that one night, we were having a revival at our church in Oak Hill. Our minister, Reverend Harold Sturm, a very special person in our family's life, was giving the invitation to turn everything over to the Lord. I remember going up front and turning my life over to the Lord. After several moments of prayer I looked up and on my right was Dan. It was a very special evening.

Dan went on to Capital University in Columbus, Ohio. He has spent his life in education starting out as a teacher and basketball coach. He has since gone into administration and is serving as Principal and Athletic Director. Three years ago he served as President of the Ohio High School Athletic Association.

In 1967, I had a problem with a parent about his son's playing time. During the week of the incident, I took some verbal abuse in the local grocery store from the gentleman. That Friday night, at a game at Coal Grove High School in Ironton, Ohio, we lost the game 75–74. I felt we were slicked at the end of the game with some bad calls that were crucial to our game.

As soon as the game ended the parent who had been giving me a hard time came down out of the stands and put his hand on my left shoulder. He said sarcastically as he was leaving "The best coach Oak Hill has ever had." I am not proud of what I did, but I hit the gentleman several times as I tore his shirt off and threw him down on the bleachers.

The athletic director of Coal Grove High School asked me if I wanted to have him arrested and I said "No, I think he already had enough." The gentleman and I never had a problem after that incident. The gentleman also happened to be the president of our Athletic Boosters Club. I remained coaching at Oak Hill for two more years.

At one game during the 1967–68 season, I started a tradition that I still practice at times with our present teams. I noticed that while the team was getting ready for a game, they just did not seem to be motivated—they seemed to be *flat*. This made me upset, and I told our manager to get me a uniform. I proceeded to don the uniform right there on the court. I told them that I would be the last man warming up, and if anyone was loafing during warm-ups my size twelve shoes would be hitting the seat of his pants. It worked! The team went out, got fired up, and won the game!

Enthusiasm Creates Momentum

My family and I loved Oak Hill very much, and we stayed there from 1962 until 1969. In 1969, it was time for a move. While job hunting, I had two interviews, including an interview for the head basketball position at Wahama, West Virginia, near Point Pleasant, and the Guernsey Catholic Central coaching and Athletic Directors positions in Cambridge, Ohio.

The superintendent at Wahama told me at the interview that the previous season the basketball coach was fired midway through the season, and that the principal took over and the team went to the West Virginia state tournament. Every player was coming back for the upcoming season. I was offered the head coaching position, as well as a job teaching, and had to serve as assistant football coach. I talked it over with my wife and we accepted. We soon rented a house in the school district, and my wife spent three days cleaning it up to get ready for our family to move in. After three days on the football field, I realized that coaching football was not for me.

Originally, I had not been hired for the Athletic Director's positions in Cambridge; it was offered to someone else. While I was (briefly) coaching football, the individual they had hired backed out. I received a call from the school in Cambridge and was offered the position. We had moved many boxes of clothes and pieces of furniture into the house at Point Pleasant, but my wife, being the special person that she is, knew I was not going to be happy as a football coach. I resigned the Wahama position and accepted the position at Cambridge. We repacked the boxes and furniture and headed for Cambridge. (Oh, by the way the superintendent at Wahama knew what he was talking about when he told me the basketball team would go back to the West Virginia state tournament. They did.)

In 1969–70 at Guernsey Catholic Central in Cambridge, Ohio, we had an extra special young man on our team. Bert McCartney was a senior my first season at the school. He scored over one thousand points in his career and went on to Findlay College.

I remember one evening that season we were playing against Indian Valley South, the score was 60–60 with one second left when Bert got fouled. He had two foul shots—he missed the first one! He looked over to our bench and smiled and calmly made the second shot for the one point win.

During our first season at Guernsey Catholic Central, we faced two important games in one weekend that I felt we had to win against two of our rivals. One game was against Parkersburg St. Joseph and the other one was against Madison High School. At the Friday afternoon pep rally, I told the student body that if we won both games that weekend, I would ride my son Jeff's twenty-inch bicycle to school on Monday morning. We beat Parkersburg St. Joseph 118–54, and Madison 95–67.

It was cold Monday morning and I had a five mile ride from our house to school. It was only fourteen degrees out and I could not find any gloves, so I put on a pair of my wife's gloves, got on the small twenty-inch bicycle, and headed for school. It took a while to get to school on that tiny bike. The bell to start the morning classes had rung, but the student body did not go in; they were waiting to see if I would keep my promise. Our principal Father Reasbeck had not attended the pep rally on Friday and could not understand why the students were not going to class. When I rode up to the school, I saw that he was out there waiting with them.

I started another trend during the 1969–70 season. I declared to both the nuns and students that whenever I felt that the game was ours and that we were going to win, I would take out my upper dentures, hold them up in the air for all to see, and then put them in my shirt pocket for the rest of the game. That signal meant that we could thank the Lord for the win.

One game, we were far ahead in the first half. The chant started early—the cheerleaders, the sisters, and the student body were cheering, "We want the teeth! We want the teeth!" I grabbed my dentures and held them up. The crowd went wild as I stuck them in my front pocket. Enthusiasm does create momentum!

The 1970–71 season gave birth to another idea that worked. Guernsey Catholic Central had never defeated Skyvue High School. At the pep rally before the Skyvue game, coaches always used the word "if." That day, I felt extra confident and did not say "if"—I said "after" we defeated Skyvue, I would walk the five miles home holding a sign that stated "G.C.C. has just defeated Skyvue!" The final score was 53–52 and it was a great night to go for a walk. Our two assistant coaches, John Smalley and Frank Parks, walked with me every step of the way.

At G.C.C., the 1969–70 season was very enjoyable. We went 14–6 on the season, losing twice to Skyvue, once to Indian Valley South by a score of 56–53, once to Stuebenville Catholic Central 68–65, and twice to Zanesville Rosecrans. While at G.C.C., I had the opportunity to coach baseball and golf at the same time. We played baseball on

Tuesdays, Thursdays and Saturdays, and golf on Mondays, Wednesdays and Fridays. Also while at G.C.C., I was employed during the summer as the city recreation director for Cambridge.

While serving as the city recreation director at Cambridge, another incident took place that I am not proud of; but I am going to be honest putting this story together, and I have to include everything that happened—not just the good, but also the bad.

We were playing a pony league baseball game at Cambridge City Park between the city's best team and Byesville's best team. Byesville athletes go to Meadowbrook High School. Cambridge and Meadowbrook are about five miles apart, so naturally they are rivals in every sport. The Cambridge newspaper's sports editor was at the game doing the article for the paper. He kept making snide comments about whoever hired the umpires for the game and complaining on how the local team was getting cheated by the umpires. It went on for a couple of innings until finally I had had enough. I walked over to him and told him I was the one who had hired the umpires and shut him up by putting a few right hooks on his left jaw. I never had another problem with that gentleman, and he called me that same evening and apologized for starting the incident.

In 1972, the recreation job became a full time job, and I was offered the position at a yearly salary of nine thousand dollars. In the meantime, a close friend of mine offered me the position of assistant basketball coach at Chillicothe High School. His name was Coach Tom Cuppett, one of the best and hardest working coaches I met in my forty-four years of coaching.

My wife and I discussed the recreation job and the coaching-teaching position at Chillicothe. We decided to ask for eleven thousand dollars a year for the recreation director job, which we did not think the Cambridge Recreation Board would offer. While we were waiting for an answer, my wife went to Chillicothe to look for a house for our family. The Recreation Board met and decided to offer me eleven thousand dollars. I called my wife at Chillicothe to let her know the good news. When she came to the phone, the first thing she said was that she had found a place for us to live and had paid the first two months rent. So we were off to Chillicothe for the next three years. I served as the assistant basketball coach under Tom Cuppett. Coach Cuppett and I go back a long way. We were classmates at Salem College, and Tom was my assistant coach at Oak Hill back in 1963 and 1964. The Chillicothe Cavaliers won the Central Ohio League Championship 1972–73 and 1973–74 seasons under Coach Cuppett, and I felt very proud that he asked me to be a part of it.

While we were at Chillicothe High School from 1972–75, we had a young man by the name of Mark Bayliss on the team. He was selected Player of the Year during the 73–74 season in the State of Ohio, and he led the Cavaliers to the Central Ohio League Championship during the 1972–73 and 1973–74 seasons. He went on to The Ohio State University and started as a freshman for Coach Fred Taylor and the Buckeyes.

In 1975, it was time to move again. In high school, I had played at Redstone High School in Republic, Pennsylvania. It had since consolidated with Brownsville High School and is now called Brownsville Area High School. I signed a three year contract to coach basketball back where I had started playing. For the 1975–76 school year, I was the Head Basketball Coach at my old high school back home in Pennsylvania. The interesting thing about this job was my high school coach was now the principal, and some of my teachers were still there teaching twenty-one years after I graduated.

During the 1975–76 season at Brownsville Area High School in Brownsville, Pennsylvania, we had a young man on the team by the name of Kenny "Budjo" Johns. He was a senior the year I coached at the school. He scored over one thousand points in his career.

The one game that I specifically remember Kenny really demonstrated his athletic ability was against Uniontown St. John's High School, which was coached by the legendary Lash Nesser. St. John's had a very good basketball team and was undefeated at the time. Vince Nesser was averaging around twenty-five points per game, and we needed to do something to shut them down. Coach Nesser's two sons were the starting guards, Vince and Steve. I had stayed up the night before the game until about three o'clock in the morning trying to figure out a way to pull off an upset.

After hours of strategizing and diagrams of X's and O's, I decided to go with a triangle-and-two combination defense. We put our three strong rebounders, Jack Durant, Ken Johns, and Kenny Thomas, in a zone defense. We then put our two guards, Jim Ashton and Poe Logan, on Vince Nesser—one on his right and one on his left. We left their other guard open with no one playing defense on him.

St. John's was averaging around 85 points per game, so on offense we were going to run a four corner stall offense. This was to slow things down, so they would not run us out of the gym, and score a hundred points. At half time, their leading scorer Vince had two points and was trying desperately to show us how good he was; he did not pass to the open man, his brother. We worked our offense to perfection, and Kenny Johns was hitting the jump shot around the foul line. He scored thirty-one points that night, and we upset St. John's 59–58. The game was definitely the highlight of our 1975–76 season. Kenny received several post season honors and went on to play at Millersville College in Pennsylvania.

Although the 1975–76 school year was very enjoyable, I sensed that my family was not happy in Brownsville, Pennsylvania. I contacted one of my players from the early days at Oak Hill, Dan Brisker, who was coaching at Canal Winchester High School near Columbus, Ohio. I explained my situation and asked him if he knew of any basketball coaching positions back in Ohio. He told me about Millersport High School, near Buckeye Lake, Ohio. During their 1975–76 season, the varsity team was 1–17 and the freshmen team went 0–12. They were coming off an 0–19 season the year before. I called the superintendent, Mr. Ed Brookover, to see if the position was open and to see if I could get an interview. I felt the Millersport position was the one I wanted because it would be a challenge, and the only way to go was up after what the team had been through the year before. Several days later, my wife, children and I packed up and piled into our station wagon, and headed for Millersport where I was to coach both the Junior varsity and varsity teams for the first year.

After the first month of the season, we had four wins and four losses. The first highlight of this season was when we were playing Danville High School. They were undefeated and ranked 15th in the state. As we stepped onto the court, I knew that a very special and exciting evening was about to unfold.

The Junior varsity game came down to the final second on the clock. The score was tied at forty-nine and it was a jump ball at our foul circle. We called time out. In our huddle, I told Mike Washburn, who was jumping against one of their shorter players, to look like he was going to tip the ball to one of the three players he was facing, but instead to tip the ball back behind him to the top of the circle to Steve Sabo. There would be no time left, so Steve had to release the shot immediately. The boys went back onto the court and executed my orders precisely. Yes, it went in at the buzzer. The final score was 51–49. How sweet it was! But that was only the beginning of a beautiful evening. The varsity game went into three overtimes. Don Waller put us ahead 73–71. At the buzzer, Danville missed a lay-up. What a gratifying evening it turned out to be! I continued coaching basketball, baseball and golf until the 1982–83 season when I was fired from all coaching duties.

To the 1979–80 teams, I made a promise back in their freshman year that if we were to defeat Liberty Union High School at Liberty Union that I would walk home. Two players did not forget that promise—Jon Mastel and John Clark reminded me in the locker room that night before the game. The game was close all the way, and with six seconds left in the game, John Clark was fouled with the score 78–77 in L.U.'s favor. He calmly made both foul shots, and we won 79–78. Our manager, Bobby Glaize, would not let me walk home alone. The walk took one hour and fifteen minutes, and it was about five miles.

Two years later we were looking forward to the upcoming season; we had four starters returning and felt this group could win the championship. But disaster hit before the season started. Jon Mastel was also our quarterback on the Laker football team and had fractured his arm at Liberty Union. Then, on the last Friday night football game versus Lancaster Fisher Catholic at Millersport, we lost John Clark and Steve Lewis to knee injuries. They were our two strongest rebounders. The other starter, Pat Sandusky, quit the team. These four starters were gone for the season. We started four sophomores and a freshman that season—Scott Zollinger, Jeff Hite, Arney Dupler, Rich Teesdale, and freshman Scott Brookover. It turned out to be a long season mainly because of the inexperience at the varsity level. But the lessons we learned during our losing season paid dividends in the next two seasons.

During the 1980–81 season, Millersport pulled off one of the biggest upsets of the year. We were playing Columbus Academy at Millersport. Our team was led by the same five players that took their lumps two years before when they were four sophomores and a freshman. The five young men who led the team that season were Scott Zollinger, Jeff Hite, Arney Dupler, Rich Teesdale, and Scott Brookover.

Scott Zollinger was a 4.0 student, an excellent leader, and was always calm. He stayed cool under pressure and never seemed to get upset. He led the state in foul shooting his junior year at ninety-one percent. Jeff White, during his senior year, was the best player in the Conference. On Friday night at Canal Winchester, he scored forty-six points and had twenty-one rebounds, and on Saturday night at Hembock Miller High School, he scored thirty-seven points and had twenty-three rebounds. Arney Dupler was a physical workhorse with an excellent shot from the corner. He was so strong and physical that some coaches thought he was always trying to hurt their players. Rich Teesdale, our point guard, was about five-foot-six and 128 pounds. He was a red-headed, fiery individual who loved to run. He was very quick and knew how to take the charge. During the 1980–81 season, he had taken fifty-four charges that were called by the officials. Scott Brookover was a junior and the fifth starter on the team. He was an excellent leaper and he had a smooth jump shot anywhere around the key.

Millersport had not won a sectional championship since the 1960–61 season when George Steele was the coach. Our goal for the 80–81 season was to win the Mid-State League Championships and a sectional Championship. Columbus Academy had a ball team that went to the State Championships that season, and ended up with a 24–2 record. But that night in Millersport, our Lakers dominated and defeated Academy by a score of 63–43. Yes, our victory was one of their two losses. And at the end of the season, our team defeated Licking Heights in the championship game and finally won a Sectional Championship that had eluded our school for twenty years.

The 1982–83 season turned out to be my last season coaching at Millersport High School. It will always be a very special year for me for several reasons. We had only six full-time varsity players on the squad. Three were seniors and three were sophomores. The three seniors were our son Brett, Mike Brumfield, and Jeff Wilhelm. The three sophomores were Dave Copeland, Perry Maughmer, and Brian Jewell. This group won thirteen games that season. Every man had to work extra hard because there was usually no one to replace him.

During the seven years I had the opportunity to coach there, there were two young men who really stood out, one being our son Brett, and the other Jeff Hite. Brett probably had the toughest time of all because he had to play for his father. As a sophomore, I kept him on the junior varsity team for half the game, and he was also the sixth man on the varsity team. This was the 1980–81 season, and I was coaching both teams without a varsity assistant coach.

I wanted to have a winning season with both teams, so I kept him as one of the leaders on the Junior varsity team. Also that season, we did have a winning record with both teams, and the varsity team went on to win the first sectional championship at the school in twenty years.

Brett's senior season he led the Mid-State League in scoring and rebounding. He was selected First Team All-Conference, First Team All-District, Central Ohio Class A Player of the Year, and First Team All-Ohio. Millersport High School retired his jersey number twelve. He went on to play his college ball at Salem College in Salem, West Virginia, where he was their leading rebounder during his sophomore, junior, and senior seasons, and was also their most valuable player. He received his Marketing and Management degree from Salem in 1988.

(One other note on his athletic ability: Two years ago in the Millersport Alumni Tournament's Championship game he scored 106 points hitting thirty of the thirty-eight three-point shots in leading his team to the championships for the fifth time.)

The other young man that excelled in basketball at Millersport was Jeff Hite. Jeff was not one of the better players on the team during his freshman year, but by the time he was a junior, he was the best player in the Mid-State League. During his senior year, he led our team to the league runner-up position, and the first sectional championship in twenty years. I have already mentioned earlier his double-double scoring and rebounding against Canal Winchester on Friday and coming back the next night versus

Miller and doing the same thing. That weekend, he scored close to eighty points, and had forty-four rebounds, which earned him Player of the Week in the Columbus area. Jeff earned First Team All-Central District and Third Team All-Ohio his senior season. He went on to Otterbein College. He had the opportunity to play in the Professional league in Europe for six seasons.

An incident occurred with a few weeks left in the 1982–83 season that cost me my coaching positions. I was serving as the head basketball coach, the head baseball coach, and head golf coach, and I was fired from all three. Our team was playing Berne Union High School at home. We were having an excellent ball game. Toward the end of the third quarter, Brett, who had scored twenty-eight points and was sitting out half of the third quarter, asked if he could go back in. He wanted to score one basket so he could hit the thirty point mark. At the time Brett was leading the Mid-State League in scoring and rebounding, and I probably should have let him stay in the game, rather than have him sit out half the third quarter. Perry Maughmer had scored eighteen points and asked to go back in to score one more basket to have twenty points. (I put both of them back in the game toward the end to score their points.)

When the game ended, the final score was Millersport—86, Berne Union—47. The Berne Union coach was upset, and thought that we had tried to run the score up on his team. He used some profanity while he was talking to our athletic director who was agreeing with him.

As my wife walked by, she overheard his comments and stopped to say, "You know John would not do that." Our athletic director told her to be quiet or she would have to leave our gymnasium. One of our players came back into the locker room and told me what was going on in the gym. I confronted the athletic director and asked him to tell me what was going on. I told him he had a choice; he could take off his glasses off or leave the gym. He started to take off his glasses, and I went after him. When we left the locker room, the Superintendent and principal were outside in the gym. I told them that I did want to hear anything they had to say.

On Monday morning, I was called in to the Superintendent's office and he told me that I would be relieved of all my coaching duties at the end of that basketball season. At the time I was very hurt, but I trusted in the Lord, and I knew things would work out. About a month after this situation occurred, Brett was named the Central Ohio Class A Player of the Year and the First Team All-Ohio, and because we had six young men who wanted to win, I was named Coach of the Year in Central Ohio.

About two weeks after I had been fired, we were scheduled to play our last home game of the season, which was also going to be my last game coaching in our gym. We were playing Fairfield Union High School out of Lancaster, Ohio. Their record at the time was seventeen wins and one loss. At the pep rally that afternoon I told the student body that since this was going to be my last game that I was going to make it a very special upset. I was going to dress in a Laker uniform and warm up with our team (incidentally, it might be the first time a father and son warmed up on the same high school team). I told them that after we won the game, I would sleep in the middle of the gym floor all night with the scoreboard lights on, so I could look at the score every time I woke up. Then in the morning I would walk home in my Laker uniform, which was about three sizes too small. Keep in mind, Fairfield Union was 17–1. We were ahead at halftime by 17 points. The final score was Millersport–86, Fairfield Union–77. Mike Brumfield scored thirty-two points with an exceptional shooting night, and our son Brett scored twenty-six points. Our fans acted like we had just won the State Championship. They cut down the nets and celebrated. It was a beautiful night to behold.

After everyone cleared out of the gym, it was time to make my bed for the night. My wife and I placed the purple gym mats at center court. We were prepared; we had our blankets and pillows with us and were ready to call it a day. She and I had done this one other time a few years earlier when we upset Amanda Clearcreek. It was a very gratifying evening. Amen!

Play the Best, Beat the Rest

After being relieved of my coaching duties at the end of the 1982–83 season, I stayed at Millersport to teach for nine years until I retired from teaching in 1992. At the end of that basketball season in 1983, our principal called me into his office one morning to let me know about a basketball coaching position that was open. He knew how much I enjoyed coaching. The position was at The Ohio State University at Newark Campus. It was only a temporary position because the head coach was taking a one year leave of absence. I was able to get an interview and I remember one of the questions I was asked was why would I want this position if it was only for one year?

My answer: "You never know what it may lead to." I was correct with that answer, as I have just finished twenty-four beautiful years of coaching basketball at ONSU-N, and have spent the last fifteen years also serving as the Athletic Coordinator at the school. I was right because the coach decided not to return. The past twenty-four years have been the most enjoyable coaching years of my forty-four.

The 1983–84 season was my first year at OSU-N. When I took over at the Newark Campus, there was only one player returning from the previous season. He was a senior and had accepted a part-time coaching position at one of the local high schools. It turned out to be an interesting experience in coaching for me because I had to find players, and we had no assistant coaches (the rest had all left after the 1982–83 season). It was a very interesting challenge—one that I could hardly wait to undertake.

Our first season, we went 4–13, but we were just beginning to rebuild the program. We made progress the next season, and our record reflected that when we went 19–10. We ended the season as the Ohio Regional Campus Conference State Runner-up.

In the State Championship game, we played Akron-Wayne College. With thirty-four seconds left in the game, the score was tied at seventy. We had possession after a turnover and decided to hold the ball and go for the last shot. We called time-out with nine seconds left to set up the final shot. We took the shot from around the foul line. The ball sailed through the air and bounced off the backboard! We missed it! Luckily we had one of our players in perfect position to grab the rebound. When he rebounded, he knew he had to rush and put the shot up quick. He did not realize that for some reason, he was all alone on the left side of the basket, and that there were two seconds on the clock.

He probably thought that the horn was going to sound ending the game, and that he was going to get fouled by someone. He missed the easy lay-up that he had made a thousand of times before, and the game ended in regulation 70–70. We were so close to pulling it off, but it was not meant to be. We lost in overtime to Akron-Wayne by a score of 88–83.

I still remember going over to Coach Smith and embracing him and congratulating him, and feeling very happy for him. I knew our turn would come. We had made progress the first two seasons. The 1986–87 season turned out to be a very rewarding experience. We had an excellent group of freshmen recruits on the team that blended in with our returning players.

When grades came out at mid-season we lost three starters with academic difficulties. It was quite a let down for the entire team including myself. The ten young men who were left decided to accept the challenge of playing without the other men. By tournament time, we were about the middle of the pack of the seventeen teams in the competition.

We made it to the Championship game against Miami Middleton. They had an excellent team and were the conference champions. We upset them both times during the regular season. It was asking quite a lot to upset them one more time.

I remember the score with one minute and fifteen seconds left in the game. Middletown had taken the lead 72–71. We called time out to talk things over. The final minute of the game went perfectly; they did not score at all and we hit two baskets. With seven seconds left, I can still remember Brad Longaberger rebounding the ball and passing to Todd Torbert at mid-court. Todd made the lay-up at the buzzer for a final score of 77–72.

That team will always be extra special. They were a group of over achievers. They would not quit. Our point guard, Rick Crabtree, was a very quick excellent ball handler and passer; that year he was the leader of the team. The other four starters were Jack Schone, Todd Torbert, Tom Foster, and Brad Longaberger. Todd Torbert was named the Most Valuable Player in the State Tournament, and Brad Longaberger was selected as the Most Valuable Player in the Conference. Brad scored 614 points that season, and Todd had 606. The young men that came off the bench to spell the starters that season were also major contributors to becoming state champions. They were Perry Mickley, Eric Cable, Scott Vermilion, Darren Foster, and Terry Rohrer. We finished that season with a 21–8 record, and to this day, they are still the only team from Newark Campus to win the Men's Basketball State Championships. We were and are very proud of them.

During the 1988–89 season, we had an important game coming up with Ohio University-Chillicothe, this time I told the team that if we were to win, I would shave my head and leave the word Titans on the back of my head. Yes, they did win it, and yes, I did shave my head.

In 1990, we decided to accept some bigger challenges outside our conference schedule. We accepted an invitation to play in the Vincennes, Indiana tournament. At that time, Vincennes University was ranked number one in the nation in the Junior College division. Also in the invitational tournament were Allegheny Community College out of Maryland (ranked ninth in the nation) and Cincinnati State. We were definitely outclassed by the other the teams, but what a beautiful challenge!

Since then, we have accepted invitations to play against some excellent competition. In 1991–92 we played Vincennes again, as well as Pikeville, Kentucky and Oakland City, Indiana. From 1990–98, we competed against several programs that we had no business being on the floor with. For example, we started out the 1996–97 season on November 10th, traveling to Georgetown, Kentucky—they were ranked pre-season at number one in the nation NAIA Division I. Two days later, we traveled north to Canton, Ohio to play Walsh University, who was ranked number two in the both the nation and the NAIA Division.

Later that season, we traveled to Nashville, Tennessee to play against David Lipscomb University; when we arrived, they were ranked number one in the nation, and they defeated Georgetown by thirty points. The other two teams at Nashville were Oklahoma City and Ohio Valley, West Virginia. Lipscomb and Oklahoma City were ranked numbers one and two at the time. Oklahoma City defeated Lipscomb in the championship game. We lost to Ohio Valley by a score of 131–97. The most important aspect of all these challenges was not the wins or losses against these excellent programs, but our lack of fear to compete against anyone, anywhere, anytime.

During the past fifteen years at OSU-N, we have had some exceptional basketball players on the team, but the one that sticks out in my mind for his achievements is Mike Dilger. Mike played high school ball at Centerburg High School. After he graduated, he decided to attend Ohio Wesleyan. He was not happy there, and I remember talking to his mother and inviting her and Mike down to our campus for a visit. I also remember telling them that if he did transfer to our program, he would have fun, score a lot of points, and graduate.

He transferred shortly after his tour. He did have fun at basketball, he did score a lot of points, and he did graduate. We were playing Ohio University-Zanesville, and Brent McLaughlin injured an ankle and could not play the second half. For this particular game, he was our sixth man and it was only his freshman season. Mike played the second half, scored twenty-six points, and we won 86–83. From that day on, he started every game. Mike played in all 112 games while at Newark Campus; he never missed a game because of illness or injury. He is now the All-time leading scorer with 1,973 points and the All-time leading rebounder with 1,134. His jersey number, thirty-two, was retired at the end of his career.

Another young man that sticks out in my mind is Todd Torbert from Licking Valley High School. Todd led our team to the only state championship back during the 1986–87 season. He was selected as the Most Valuable Player in the state tournament that season. During his career, he scored 1,570 points, which ranks him second behind Mike Dilger. His jersey number, twelve, was also retired at the end of his career.

The last young man I would like to mention is Rob Smith from Lakewood High School. He was our point guard for three and a half seasons. He was exceptionally quick and enjoyed passing the ball to his teammates more than scoring. However, he did score 1,298 points during his career and his jersey number, ten, was retired

I remember one game at Ohio University Chillicothe during his senior season. We were trailing in the game 97–96 with about twenty seconds left in the game, and Chillicothe had the ball. They took a shot they did not need to take. Mike Dilger got the rebound, and passed it to Rob on the fast break. As he was dribbling at mid-court, there were five seconds left in the game, and as a good coach, I knew I had to call a timeout. I was on my feet and ready to call the timeout, but something told me to shut up. I could see in Rob's eyes as he went by me that he was taking the ball to the basket. As he released the shot, the buzzer sounded, and the ball went into the basket for the 98–97 victory. He scored thirty-one points that game. The only three jersey numbers that have been retired at Ohio State University Newark Campus belonged to Mike Dilger, Todd Torbert, and Rob Smith.

After thirty-five years of coaching and fifty years of either playing or coaching basketball, it was time to give some thought to retiring from coaching doing something else with my life. I met with my supervisor at the University, Mr. David Thomson, the Director of Student Support Services. I told him that I wanted to write a book about some of my experiences in coaching, and I was giving thoughts to giving up my coaching duties, but staying on as Athletic Coordinator. Incidentally, I have tried to retire from coaching three other times, and almost did.

We discussed my situation and he helped me make a very important decision. Dr. Rafael Cortada, our President, and Mr. Thomson approved my request to take a year-long leave of absence from my coaching duties, finish my book, and decide what my future would be in coaching.

They also let me hire an interim coach for the 1997–98 season while I was working on my book. I wanted my interim coach to be a person I knew could not only handle the job, but do it well. He did just that. The interim coach just happened to be our son Brett. He instituted a very rigorous conditioning program during preseason. After conditioning, he had the athletes run two miles before the day's work was complete. The important thing about the run was that he led the way, and he was always the first man back to the gym. I was very appreciative of how he handled the coaching duties. He was also fortunate to have a good assistant coach, a volunteer, who just happened to be his father-in-law.

At the start of the 1998–99 school year, I got back in the game, and I was looking forward to the upcoming season for several reasons. One was to find out if I could still stand the grind of the four and a half months of practices and games. Another reason was to find out if I still had the enthusiasm that I had had the past thirty-five years. But probably the most important reason was stupid and selfish on my part. I did not want Brett to be a coach at this time of his life. He had just received a promotion at State Farm Insurance Company to fire claims superintendent. He and his wife Jennifer seemed to be very happy, and he still enjoyed playing the game at age thirty-three. I felt that the stress and pressure that I had put on myself all these years was one thing I did not want him to go through. As I said earlier, it was very stupid and selfish on my part, but it was too late for me to walk away and change it.

We started tryouts for the team the first week of October. A young man from Las Vegas had played the previous season for Brett. He did well in school academically his first year and when he returned in 1998, brought three of his friends from Las Vegas. He had talked to them when he went home for the summer and they decided to transfer to our school. One of the young men had played the previous season at a Division I school, Southern Utah, and the other two were also very strong and skilled basketball players.

It was very unusual for our program, but after the very first practice, we knew who our starting five would be. We only had two players returning to the program from the previous season, so everything and every position looked wide open. After the very first practice we could see that the four young men from Las Vegas and our shooting guard from Cleveland Brush High School were our starters, and we had a six-foot-six freshman from Pickerington High School, and a six-foot-five freshman from Tri-Valley High School as our seven players. It looked to be one of the better groups of athletes that we had in the past sixteen years at Newark Campus.

We had put a very tough schedule together for the season, playing five games with teams that were what we called "scholarship schools." Salem-Teiyko University in Salem, West Virginia was an NCAA Division II school, and in the 1996–97 season, they had played in the NCAA Division II National Championship game. They were ranked number one in their conference for the previous three seasons. Their 1997–98 record was 34–2. They were well out of our class, but we accepted the challenge. We also played Alderson Broaddus College from Phillpé, West Virginia. They had an excellent program. They had defeated Salem Teiyko during the previous season and we were scheduled to play them twice.

We also accepted an invitation to participate in the Milligan College Tournament at Johnson City, Tenn. Year in and year out, Milligan always has as strong program, and the past few seasons, they had been ranked in the top ten in the NAIA. Also in the Milligan College Tournament were teams from Cumberland College, Kentucky and Warren Wilson, North Carolina. We knew that it would take a major upset for us to win any of these five non-conference games, but we were ready for the challenge. One of our mottos for the upcoming season was "Play the Best and Beat the Rest."

Looking back now that the season is over, we lost all five of those games—three of them very convincingly. One of those losses was to Salem Teiyko University 118–59, another to Milligan 124–79, and the third to Alderon Broaddus 104–69. We lost the other game to Alderson Broaddus, 104–88, and were down twelve points with two minutes left in the game and missed two easy lay-ups. Our only chance to upset one of the big dogs, as I put it to the team, was at the Milligan College Tournament.

We trailed Warren Wilson, North Carolina by twenty-two points late in the first half, and it looked like they were going to run us out of the gym. With thirty-three seconds left in the game, we scored on a fast break lay-up to go ahead 71–69. With seventeen seconds left in the game, it was tied at seventy-one, and we had the ball and missed an easy lay-up, and they went down and scored off two foul shots. Trailing 71–73 with five seconds left, our shooting guard, with his quickness, beat his man, but missed the uncontested lay-up. Our six-foot-six post player got the rebound, but missed the last shot at the buzzer. The final score was 71–73, but we knew we could compete when we got back to our conference schedule.

We went back home to open our conference schedule against Miami Hamilton; they were the defending champions. We lost to them by a score of 106–93. We had our chances for the upset, but it did not happen. Their team was even stronger and better than the team that won the conference the year before. To attest to that, they ended up the 1998–99 season by going 18–0, winning the conference and also winning the State Championship.

After that game, we proceeded to win the next four conference games. After five games, we were 4–1. We were in second place behind Miami Hamilton and felt good about our chances. By then, the end of Autumn Quarter was approaching, which was also when the athletes' grades were checked. I waited anxiously to see how many players we would be losing because of academic problems. We demand and enforce a 2.0 grade point average for an athlete to continue playing in our program for the last half of the season. During the previous fifteen seasons, this policy had really affected our program. On average, we lost three players every season because of grade difficulties. The previous season, when Brett was our head coach, the team lost five players when grades came out. So I was prepared and expected the worst.

From the start of the 98–99 season, of the original twelve players selected (and, as I mentioned earlier, probably the most talent we had assembled for our basketball program), we were left with five. Before we even stepped foot on the court for a game, one of the players quit. He and I met, and I always make each of the players know where they stand in our scheme of things as far as playing time is concerned. After our discussion, he decided to quit the team; we both felt that he made the right decision because he was getting ready to graduate, working, and carrying a full schedule of courses. Basketball would not have been his number one priority.

The Division I player from Las Vegas and Southern Utah only played in one game the first half of the season. He felt that once he arrived in Newark, the city was not for him. He did not want to stay and asked me to help find him an athletic scholarship elsewhere. In the single game that he played for us, he scored twenty-two points, and had eight rebounds in only playing about twenty minutes, or half of the game. His grade point average after the autumn quarter would not have allowed him to continue playing the last half of the season anyway. He left for the New Orleans area after the quarter was over.

We also lost our backup point guard and our six-foot-six post player because of grades, and the six-foot-five post player quit the team because he was working a full-time job and carrying a full-time schedule. The other two players from Las Vegas that came in for the season had financial problems at the start of winter quarter. They could not obtain any loans or financial aid whatsoever. Winter quarter classes started on January 4th, and they both had to drop out of school on the 5th. Losing those two fine young men and excellent basketball players really hurt what was left of the team. One of them, Tomay Holdrys, was leading the conference in scoring with twenty-three points per game, and he was also first in rebounding averaging eleven rebounds per game. The other young man, Brodrick Ivory, was averaging eighteen points per game, and nine rebounds per game.

Despite our losses, we knew it was time to find a few more players to continue on with the second half of the season. We added three more players to the roster and finished the season with eight. A few interesting things happened during the latter part of this season. Akron Wayne College had already defeated us twice—once at their place by a score of 88–80, and again in a Holiday Tournament by a score of 102–85. We were getting ready to play them again, and on the day of the game, I had an important conversation with our shooting guard from Cleveland Brush High School. He was averaging twelve points per game at the time.

Jokingly I said, "Marticé we need someone to step up the scoring burden to help our team win."

That evening, he scored forty-eight points, and we won by a score of 103–93. Another important occurrence happened during the game with six minutes and forty-five seconds left in the game. The score was tied. Marticé drove to the basket and collided with one of the Akron players. He was down on the floor injured, but the official near the basket did not blow his whistle and make the call. I felt he should have called a blocking foul on their player or a charge on our player; either way, he should have called something.

As I walked on to the floor to see how serious Marticé's injury was, I looked at the official and calmly asked him, "When was the last time you went to Lens Crafters to have your eyes checked. Obviously, you cannot see."

Yes, he did give me a technical foul and proceeded to tell me that if I did not settle down, he was going to give me another one, and eject me from the game. I noticed the smirk on his face and I knew that the satisfaction he would get by throwing me out would have made his day.

I looked him in the eyes and told him, "Sir I cannot let you do that. I am going to throw myself out. Have a nice day." As I strode out of the gymnasium, I knew that Brett would take care of everything. He pulled off the upset. Amen!

Our next game was against Ohio State-Lima. They had defeated us once in the first half of the season by a score of 97–71. On the day of the game, I saw Marticé walking in the gym lobby and again jokingly asked him if he could score forty-eight again that evening.

He was a very quiet young man, but he looked at me and said, "Yes!" He scored fifty points that evening, tying our school scoring record which is also held by Steve Gilbert from Heath High School. We lost that game by a score of 106–102, but celebrated for Marticé's victory.

We had defeated Ohio University-Lancaster earlier in the season 85–82, and they defeated us in the Holiday Tournament by a score of 94–81. During our next game against them, Marticé (who was now our leading scorer) had twenty points in the first half. Six minutes into the second half, he questioned a no-call by an official. He received a technical foul, and he made a remark to the other official, who gave him a second technical foul. He was ejected from the game for those two technical fouls and was forced to leave the gymnasium.

When I went to talk to the official to find out what had happened, he looked at me and smiled. He informed me that he was going to throw me out on the first technical foul he gave me. I had encountered this situation once before and knew exactly how I would handle it.

Once again, I found myself saying, "Sir I cannot let you do that." I continued, "I have had enough of your officiating tonight so I am just going to leave." I did, and I had perfect confidence in my associate coach. Yes, we did win the game by a score of 114–98. My only regret is that I probably should have thrown myself out of a few more games. I did it twice, and our team won both times.

The last highlight of the year took place in the last two weeks of the regular season. On February 6th, we were playing our last conference game at Ohio University Eastern. They manhandled us by a score of 109–69. It was a very embarrassing afternoon. On February 20th, we were scheduled to play in the Ohio Regional Campus Conference State Tournament. Once again, we were to meet Ohio University-Eastern on the court. I had already announced my retirement from coaching, which would take place after we were eliminated from the tournament.

During the pre-game warm-ups on of the Eastern players came over to shake my hand. He said that he heard that I was retiring, and that this would be my last game. He let the last statement slip, and I could see he meant no insult.

I thanked him and said, "You never know we may win."

I think that their over confidence may have been an important factor in our favor.

The final score was in our favor 95–92. It was a very rewarding day for me knowing that our young men never gave up after all they had been through during the season. After their hard work and all the effort they had put in, I honestly did not care what happened the rest of the tournament. That game against Ohio University Eastern will stick in my mind for a long time.

The next day of the tournament, we had to play the defending State Champion, Cincinnati Clermont. They were well coached and excellent athletes. They defeated us that afternoon by a score of 96–64, and I figured my coaching career at OSU-N had come to an end.

Not Finished Yet!

As the 1999–2000 school year started, we hired a coach to replace me, and I looked forward to being the school's Athletic Director with no coaching duties at all. It came time for the basketball season to get underway, and the women's team got started first. They played in an invitational tournament on November 5th and 6th at Mount Vernon Nazarene. In their first game, they played the host, the Mt. Vernon Nazarene team. At half-time, we were behind by only one point at 27–28. In the second half, our opponents made some adjustments; we did not. Our Ladies ended up losing by a score of 78–53.

The next day in the consolation game against a strong Berea, Kentucky, we lost by a score of 70–60. During both games, I noticed that the team did not seem prepared and looked very unhappy. The coach appeared unenthusiastic and did not give the impression that he was really *in* either game. The Monday after the tournament, two of the leaders on the team walked into my office.

"Coach K," they said, "something has to be done. We are all ready to quit the team." They told me that the team was not prepared for the games that past weekend and that the coach never seemed to care and never made a move to help prepare them. For them, the practices were a waste of time.

I decided to talk to the head coach and to everyone on the team. When the coach and I met, I relayed to him the problems I heard. I informed him that I was going to talk to members of the team individually and then get back to him to discuss what could be done to help the program. After meeting with all nine of the team members, and seeing that every member had negative feelings about their team and their coach, I felt that the only answer was to ask the coach to resign before the program was lost. Not one single player had anything positive to say about their preparation, practices, or even their coach's attitude.

I met with my supervisor, the Director of Student Support Services at Newark Campus, and told him of my decision to ask the coach to resign, and asked for his advice and permission to do it. On November 8, 1999, I talked to the coach and asked for his resignation. I told him that he was about to lose his team, and the schedule would have to be cancelled if nothing was done. After some discussion, he turned over his keys and left.

The next day, I met with the team and the assistant coach to make myself clear to them that I was taking over the duties as their head coach for the remainder of the season. At the time I was not sure what impact the decision would have on the team. But as the season progressed, I could see that the decision was definitely the right one. The team ended up the season with a 14–0 record in the Ohio Regional Campus Conference, reigning as the undefeated Conference Champions. They went on to win the State Championship by defeating three exceptional teams. In the Miami Hamilton game, we won 82–63; against Akron Wayne, the defending State Champion, we won by a score of 75–57; and finally, we defeated Ohio State-Lima in the Championship game by a score of 91–61. Overall, the team finished the season after the 0–2 start with a final record of twenty-three wins and three losses. Needless to say, it was one of the most enjoyable seasons I ever had the privilege to coach.

The most satisfying thing to see was the smiles on each and every player's face at the conclusion of the final game. The decision that I made on November 8, 1999 was the correct decision.

I continued to coach our women's team for the next two seasons. In the 2000–01 season, we were once again the ORCC State Champions and the ORC Conference Champions. Our record was 13–1 in the Conference and 19–2 overall. During the 2001–02 season, we finished at 15–9 overall. We were ORCC State Runners-up, losing to Miami Middletown in the championship game by a score of 51–37. We also ended up being ORC Conference Runner-up.

The next season, I resumed the head coaching position with our Men's program. The 2004–05 season was a very rewarding season at 18–13. We went to the Final Four in the State Tournament, but lost to Cincinnati Clermont in the semi-finals. They went on to become State Champions.

The 2004–05 school year also produced our first All Sports awards honor in twenty years. Our Women's volleyball team came in first, our baseball and golf teams came in second place, and our Women and Men's basketball teams came in third place. This gave us the overall point total of seventy-eight points compared to Miami Hamilton's sixty-nine points.

On November 18, 2006, we were playing Glenville State, a NCAA Division II school in West Virginia. We were very close to pulling off a major upset; we were down three points with two minutes left but ended up losing 95–85.

My wife and I were spending the night in a motel in Clarksburg, West Virginia. At about three o'clock in the morning, she awoke and became very sick. I called 9–1–1 and the Bridgeport Washington emergency squad responded and took her to the local hospital. It seemed ironic to me that she was at the local hospital for this emergency, considering that this was the same hospital where she had our first two children forty-six and forty-four years earlier.

The diagnosis was a mild heart attack and double pneumonia besides her emphysema. The doctors were not optimistic that she would be able to recover. She was put on a life support system for a week and a half. The Lord did get her through it, and after two weeks in the Clarksburg hospital, I had her transferred to The Ohio State University Hospital in Columbus, Ohio, which is only thirty miles from our home. They were going to fly her from West Virginia to Columbus, but that day, the wind was too strong. After waiting all day, they made the decision to transport her by ambulance at about nine o'clock at night. This was a four hour trip and she had to be put back on a life support system to make the trip.

After arriving at University Hospital in Columbus, she was put into the Intensive Care Unit, and remained on life support for the next eight days. Altogether, she spent thirteen days in the West Virginia hospital and fourteen days in University Hospital. She was released to the Arlington Care Center in Newark on December 21st for rehabilitation and stayed there for thirteen days. I finally was able to take her home on January 3, 2007.

During her hospitalization, Dave Chaconas, who was one of our players, took the duties as interim coach until I could return. I was able to return to our team once my wife was in the Care Center in Newark, which is only one mile from the college. I knew once I was able to get my wife home that I would no longer be able to coach the team. My last game was December 21, 2006, and our team responded by winning 93–85 at Ohio University-Lancaster.

On January 3, 2007, I submitted my resignation as coach, and one of our former players from fifteen years ago, Rob Smith, took over the team, and he did an exceptional job during the remainder of the season. When I resigned, we were 10–7 overall and 4–4 in our conference. Coach Smith went 10–5 and the team ended up with a record of 20–12 overall and 11–7 in our conference, which was good enough for third place.

I AM NOT FINISHED YET! I WILL COACH AGAIN!

I am still serving as Athletic Director at The Ohio State University Campus. This year, I am starting my forty-fifth year in education, and, of course, I am still having fun. I also serve as the Physical Education Director at the college. I will not be coaching basketball this coming season because of my wife's health, but I will return to coaching in a couple of years when we get her condition improved.

I am going to consider retiring from coaching when I turn ninety-two years of age. Many coaches will have more wins, but not many coaches will have done it for sixty-five years. My wife has already promised me that when the Lord calls me home, I will be wearing my coaching shirt, pants, and basketball shoes, and I will have a basketball tucked under my arm. They will be playing two songs at the viewing: *Sweet Georgia Brown* and *The Old Rugged Cross*. There will be a sign above the casket, and it will read:

SMILE—COACH K HAS FINALLY MADE THE LORD'S HALL OF FAME!

I would like to close by mentioning my beautiful family:

My wife of forty-eight years, Karen, whom I told on our first date that we were going to get married. The Lord gave us three beautiful children: Rebecca (Becky), Jeffrey, and Brett, and our grandchildren: Jennifer (age 24), Justin (age 19), April (age 16), Savanna (age 15), Kinley (age 1) and Jordan Brett, who was born July 26, 2007.

Epilogue

Our daughter Becky now lives about a block away from us with her two children Justin "Bull" Miller, who is nineteen, and April Lynn, who is sixteen. She has grown up to be just like her mother, a very thoughtful person, worrying about everyone but herself. She works at the Millersport Pharmacy.

Our son Jeff lives in Winter Springs, Florida, which is near Orlando. He is married to Jo Ellen Wissinger Kaminsky, and they have a daughter Jennifer Renee, age twenty-four. Jeff owns a landscape and lawn business in Florida.

Our other son, Brett lives in Heath, Ohio with his wife the former Jennifer Wright, and daughters Savanna and Kinley. Brett is a Superintendent of fire claims at State Farm Insurance. They now own and operate two Noah's Ark daycare programs—one in Newark and one in Heath.